Ours to Share

COEXISTING IN A CROWDED WORLD

KARI JONES

WITHDRAWN

ORCA BOOK PUBLISHERS

Text copyright © 2019 Kari Jones

All rights reserved. No part of this publication may be reproduced or transmitted in any form or by any means, electronic or mechanical, including photocopying, recording or by any information storage and retrieval system now known or to be invented, without permission in writing from the publisher.

Library and Archives Canada Cataloguing in Publication

Jones, Kari, 1966–, author
(Orca footprints)

Description: Series statement: Footprints series | Includes bibliographical references and index.

Identifiers: Canadiana (print) 20190076666 | Canadiana (ebook) 20190076747 | ISBN 9781459816343 (hardcover) | ISBN 9781459816350 (PDF) | ISBN 9781459816367 (EPUB)

Subjects: LCSH: Population—Environmental aspects—Juvenile literature. | LCSH: Overpopulation—Juvenile literature. | LCSH: Human ecology—Juvenile literature. | LCSH: Social ecology—Juvenile literature. | LCSH: Sustainability—Juvenile literature. | LCSH: Natural resources—Management—Juvenile literature. | LCSH: Environmental protection—Juvenile literature.

Classification: LCC HB849.415.J66 2019 | DDC j304.2—dc23

Library of Congress Control Number: 2019934046
Simultaneously published in Canada and the United States in 2019

Summary: Part of the nonfiction Footprints series for middle readers, illustrated with color photographs. Examines how overpopulation leads to unequal sharing of the Earth's social and natural resources.

Orca Book Publishers is committed to reducing the consumption of nonrenewable resources in the making of our books. We make every effort to use materials that support a sustainable future.

Orca Book Publishers gratefully acknowledges the support for its publishing programs provided by the following agencies: the Government of Canada, the Canada Council for the Arts and the Province of British Columbia through the BC Arts Council and the Book Publishing Tax Credit.

The author and publisher have made every effort to ensure that the information in this book was correct at the time of publication. The author and publisher do not assume any liability for any loss, damage or disruption caused by errors or omissions. Every effort has been made to trace copyright holders and to obtain their permission for the use of copyrighted material. The publisher apologizes for any errors or omissions and would be grateful if notified of any corrections that should be incorporated in future reprints or editions of this book.

Front cover photos: Shutterstock.com, Stocksy.com
Back cover image: Shutterstock.com

Edited by Sarah N. Harvey
Design and production by Teresa Bubela and Jenn Playford

ORCA BOOK PUBLISHERS
orcabook.com

Printed and bound in China.

22 21 20 19 • 4 3 2 1

Sharing our world starts with caring for people and animals. KONGJONGPHOTOSTOCK/ISTOCK.COM

To Mira, because you inspire me

Contents

CHAPTER ONE: SHAPING THE WORLD

CHAPTER TWO: SHARING THE WORLD

CHAPTER THREE:
WHOSE WORLD IS THIS?

CHAPTER FOUR:
SHARING OUR LIVES

Introduction

People and animals interact in all kinds of places. CALVIN QIANG

This is me (at right) all dressed up for a fundraiser to support refugees. MICHAEL STEWART

Last year I was woken up one morning by a loud noise coming from across the street. An old house that had been there for more than fifty years was being knocked down. Over the next few months three houses were built on that lot. The same thing happened down the street, only this time a small house was replaced by an apartment building. What was happening?

I started paying more attention, and I noticed that everywhere I looked, single buildings were being torn down and replaced by building complexes. Throughout the city, new roads were being paved and subdivisions built in areas that until recently had been forest or open lands. In the past few years I have noticed there is more traffic, schools have more portables, and parks and playgrounds are always busy. Wildlife that used to live entirely in the forests is now finding its way into urban neighborhoods.

This trend is happening everywhere, not just in my city. All around the world, as the human population grows, things are getting more crowded. I asked myself, How can so many people live together and share the world with other species too? Whose world is this? And how are we going to share it?

From the top of the Empire State Building all you can see is New York City.
MYKOLA LUKASH/DREAMSTIME.COM

CHAPTER ONE

Shaping the World

FROM AN ALIEN'S EYES

Imagine you live on a planet far from Earth. What would you see if you traveled through space and landed on one of our continents? This is a question I sometimes ask myself, and my answer is always the same: you'd see people, or at least evidence of human activity. Our cities are full of human-built structures, our farmlands have machinery scattered across them, and even our wildernesses have roads crisscrossing them and airplanes flying over them. There's hardly any place left on Earth that is untouched by humans. It wasn't always like that.

The Map Rock in Idaho, made about 12,000 years ago, showed people how to find water.
BOISE STATE UNIVERSITY LIBRARY, MSS 80 254/ WIKIPEDIA.ORG

MAPPING THE WORLD

Since long before there were written words, people have been using maps to explain our relationship with the world around us. Luckily for us, some of those early maps still exist. We can use them to learn how our ancestors moved across the world.

There are traces of people all around the globe. BRUCE ROLFF/SHUTTERSTOCK.COM

Throughout the ancient world, in places like Babylon and Sumeria (in what is now called Iraq), maps were used to show people where it was safe to be, where water ran, where minerals could be found or which fields were fertile. They also showed unsafe places, like where a volcano might erupt or where wild animals lived.

These early maps painted a picture of a world that is much different than it is today. It is impossible for historians to know exactly how many people there were in the world 12,000 years ago, but most estimates say there were about one million. That sounds like a lot, but if you think of a person as a single drop of water, a million people is only about ten gallons (thirty-eight liters) of water. That's about the size of a large plant pot.

With only one million people on Earth, most of it was uninhabited by humans. People huddled together in small groups to protect themselves from animals and the elements.

DENSITY FACT: The most famous ancient map is the Babylonian Imago Mundi from 660 BCE, which shows the city of Babylon and the seven cities around it on the Euphrates River in what is now Iraq.

Being together brought safety and made hunting and gathering easier. People were less likely to be eaten by wild animals or to die of starvation or thirst. It must have been tough being human 12,000 years ago. There were so many dangers out in the big world.

MOVING IN

One way early humans made life easier for themselves and their families was to share their lives and their houses with other species. Anthropologists think wolves were likely the first *domesticated* animals. Perhaps an early human child found a wolf cub and brought it home. Wolves live in packs, and a cub would quickly learn to treat its human family as its pack. Having a wolf as part of your family would make hunting animals like deer and caribou easier, and it would be good for the wolf too, because it would get regular meals and a warm fire to curl up next to at night.

Domesticating animals may have started with wolves, but it didn't stop there. Over time people began keeping animals for food and labor. Living in close company with animals and

Children like these kids in Kyrgyzstan have been riding donkeys since the animals were first domesticated, around 3000 BCE.
OLGA LABUSOVA/DREAMSTIME.COM

Shared Lives

When my husband and I were traveling in Northern Australia, we came across an ancient map high up in the hills. At first we didn't know what it was, but the more we looked at it, the more we were able to see the lines etched into the rock. The artists who had drawn the map also left their handprints on the rock. I put my hand above the red print, and even though I could never know who the artist was, I felt like we were touching each other over the centuries.

My friends and I standing next to a wall with paintings on it.
PHOTO COURTESY OF KARI JONES

breeding them for particular traits eventually led to the animals we know today: dogs, sheep, cows, pigs, chickens.

Imagine how much easier life became when you could walk out the door and milk a cow or gather some chicken eggs from the barn rather than having to hunt down a wild animal for food. Because animals were being domesticated, people found they had less need to hunt and gather their food and could settle into small farming communities or villages. From about 6,000 years ago, when there were approximately four million humans in the world, people also started using oxen, buffalo and other cattle to help them plow fields, which made growing grains and vegetables easier. People ate better and lived longer, thanks to their animals. Over the next centuries humans learned how to domesticate horses, camels, rabbits and even silk moths and bees.

Life became easier for farmers when they had animals to help with the work. In Myanmar, farmers still plow the land with the ancient method of using oxen.
VLADIMIR MELNIK/SHUTTERSTOCK.COM

GATHERING TOGETHER

As the human population of the world grew, so did the communities people lived in. The first communities were made up of small family groups, but over time unrelated families banded together in order to share the work of farming and raising animals. Eventually small villages were born. In 3500 BCE there were about 18 million people on earth. If we think about people as drops of water again, that's about 180 gallons (680 liters) of water, close to what four large bathtubs would hold. With all these people in the world, it made sense that the communities they lived in were growing too.

These ruins are all that remain of the great city of Uruk. ANDY HOLMES/WIKIPEDIA.ORG

Small villages grew into towns, which grew into cities. It's hard to say where the first cities were. Archeologists have found remnants of ancient cities in many places around the world, but many agree that the first city was Uruk in what is now Iraq. It was founded by King Enmerkar sometime around 4500 BCE, and it is the first place we know of where people built houses and other buildings out of stone.

Unfortunately, there is not much left of the ancient city of Babylon, but archeological records tell us how important the city was.

UNITED STATES NAVY 030529-N-5362A-001/ WIKIPEDIA.ORG

DENSITY FACT: The earliest known evidence of a domesticated dog is a 1,200-year-old jawbone found in a cave in Iraq.

The ancient city of Babylon was well organized. It was known for its fabulous hanging gardens. This hand-colored engraving, probably made in the 19th century after the first excavations in the Assyrian capital, depicts the fabled hanging gardens, with the Tower of Babel in the background.

MARTEN VAN HEEMSKERCK/WIKIPEDIA.ORG

Living in a city had many advantages. Trade was easier because there was usually a central gathering space where merchants could set up their stalls or shops. Large structures could be built to store crops and water. Art and science also flourished in cities. The ancient city of Babylon was well known for its glassmaking and was a center for astrology, physics, mathematics, literature, law and architecture. Many ancient cities had walls around them to keep the people inside safe from invaders and wild animals such as wild boars, lions and bears that threatened both people and their domesticated animals. The city of Jericho had a forty-foot (twelve-meter) wall surrounding it. According to the Bible, the walls of Jericho fell after Joshua's Israelite army marched around the city, blowing their trumpets. Archeological excavations have failed to produce data to substantiate the biblical story.

HUMANS EVERYWHERE!

As time went on, more and more humans crowded into cities, so that 4,000 years ago most cities were bursting at the seams. Uruk, which had started out with between 150 and 300 inhabitants, had grown to 40,000 to 50,000 residents.

Historians estimate that 2,000 years ago there were over 200 million people living in the world. In 10,000 years the Earth's population went from the equivalent of ten gallons (thirty-eight liters) of water droplets to that of more than 300 Olympic-sized swimming pools.

GROWING PAINS

The growing human population caused problems for many cities. In some places there wasn't enough water to support the number of people who lived there. Fields and gardens wilted, making food hard to come by. Materials for building new houses became scarce, and people started stealing building materials from each other. Traffic jams of horse-drawn carriages and carts clogged the central cities. Garbage and sewage piled up, and there was nowhere to put it. Imagine how dirty and stinky the ancient cities were!

Eventually people abandoned these cities in favor of places where they could find fields to work and better lives for their families. Many of the great cities of antiquity are no longer inhabited, from Uruk and Babylon to the Mayan city of Copan in South America to many great Chinese cities. It turned out that sharing with neighbors in crowded cities was hard to do.

CHANGING THE WORLD

Humans have always adapted their environments. On the west coast of Canada there is evidence that *Indigenous peoples* created

There are people everywhere. In some cities there are so many people it seems like it would be impossible to get away from the crowds. RUBYRASCAL/ISTOCK.COM

Shared Lives

A friend of mine lives on a sheep farm in northern British Columbia. When we visited, we watched the dogs round up the sheep by herding them down the field into a pen. The dogs were very good at their jobs, and the sheep all made it into the pen safely. There was another dog on the farm, and when I asked what his job was my friend told me that the dog protected the farm from bears. Every night he walked around the perimeter of the farm, and when he saw or sniffed a bear, he barked loudly and scared the bear away. That night we heard the dog barking, and I knew we were safe.

Akbash dogs were one of the earliest breeds to be trained to protect sheep from predators.
MIKEROGAL/ISTOCK.COM

The west coast of Canada is not the only place where fishing weirs have been used for centuries. These fishermen in the Democratic Republic of Congo use a similar method. JULIEN HARNEIS/WIKIPEDIA.ORG

Now that Sudan has died, there is no longer any hope that the northern white rhino population can recover. MAKE IT KENYA/STUART PRICE/WIKIPEDIA.ORG

stone weirs (barriers) underwater to channel salmon into areas where they could be caught more easily. They also created clam beds and cultivated camas bulbs to eat and trade. In Australia Indigenous peoples burned forests to create grasslands for their animals to graze on.

But as the human population of the world grew, so did the impact people had on the land. After the *Industrial Revolution*, a period of major industrialization that took place during the late 1700s and early 1800s, this impact accelerated. More and more forests gave way to crops, rivers were rerouted by dams, mountaintops were blown off for mining, and grasslands were covered by roads. By the early 1900s human enterprise had taken over so much of the globe that land had to be put aside to make sure that some wilderness remained. In 1922 Aldo Leopold of the United States Forest Service proposed that the headwaters of the Gila River be protected from development. On June 3, 1924, the Gila Wilderness in New Mexico became the world's first protected wilderness area. Currently less than 20 percent of the world's key *biodiversity* areas are completely covered by protected areas.

RIPPLE EFFECT

The boom in human population has had an impact on many animals and ecosystems. Pollution and development have destroyed habitats for many species. Scientists say that in the past 500 years more than 1,000 species have become extinct. Many species of bears, lions, tigers, elephants, rats, shrews, herons, parrots, ducks and other animals are long gone from the world. This includes ones that used to roam the world in vast numbers. The passenger pigeon, once the most abundant bird in North America, dwindled from billions (yes, billions) of birds to just one, a bird named Martha who died on September 1, 1914. Sudan, the last remaining male northern white rhinoceros, died on March 20, 2018, leaving only two female northern white rhinos in the world.

Many years ago, when a friend of mine was working outdoors in northern British Columbia, she felt a thundering under her feet. She wondered what on earth it could be, so she climbed to the top of a nearby hill. When she looked down she saw thousands of caribou crossing a river below. She sat and watched the animals for hours. Now this same herd of caribou, known as the Gray Ghosts, is down to three animals, all female. It's a sad ending for this species, but thankfully there are many examples of animals being brought back from the brink of extinction by determined groups of *conservationists*. For more information about endangered species and the work being done to save them, read *Gone Is Gone: Wildlife under Threat* by Isabelle Groc.

Today we still have to worry about species going extinct, including the once abundant caribou. JEFF439/ISTOCK.COM

THE SHAPE OF THE WORLD TODAY

A map of today's world tells a completely different story than a map of the ancient world. While once a few human habitations huddled together for safety in untouched spaces, there are now people sprawled across the globe. By 1804 there were one billion people in the world. By 1927 there were two billion. In 1960 there were three billion. Now there are almost eight billion of us. People aren't drops of water in bathtubs or swimming pools anymore; they are drops of water in an ever-expanding lake.

So how are we going to share this world of ours?

La Paz, Bolivia, is built up the side of a mountain. It is one of the highest cities in the world. PADCHAS/ISTOCK.COM

DENSITY FACT: Historians think Rome was the largest city in the world 2,000 years ago, with a population of about one million. That's about the size of present-day Tucson, Arizona, or Edmonton, Alberta.

CHAPTER TWO

Sharing the World

Eleanor Roosevelt holding the United Nations Universal Declaration of Human Rights. FRANKLIN D ROOSEVELT LIBRARY
WEBSITE/WIKIPEDIA.ORG

IT'S OUR RIGHT

The United Nations Universal Declaration of Human Rights says that we are all born free and equal, and that everyone has the right to housing, food and other things that make our lives healthy and secure. But when we look around the world, we see many social and environmental problems that stop people from accessing their fair share of resources and opportunities.

GO SWEDEN!

Overpopulation is a major cause of many of the environmental and social problems we face in the world today. It makes sense. If one person dumps garbage on the ground it's not a big deal, but if everyone does we have a garbage problem.

The Fresh Kills landfill on Staten Island in New York was so big it could be seen from space. At its peak it was receiving 13,000 tons of garbage a day. And it was just one of millions of landfills around the world. About 10 percent of the world's plastics end up in the ocean, causing over a million seabirds and 100,000 marine mammals to die every year because they mistake plastics for food.

Fortunately there are solutions to the garbage problem. In Sweden garbage is used to create energy. They've done such a good job recycling and burning waste that only one percent of their garbage ends up in landfills. In fact, Swedes have become so good at recycling and burning waste that they've run out of garbage and now have to import it from other countries to make energy.

You can sell your plastic waste at a recycling machine at Coop supermarket in Karlstad City, Sweden. APPLEYAYEE/SHUTTERSTOCK.COM

UNITED NATIONS UNIVERSAL DECLARATION OF HUMAN RIGHTS, ARTICLE 25

(1) Everyone has the right to a standard of living adequate for the health and well-being of himself and of his family, including food, clothing, housing and medical care and necessary social services, and the right to security in the event of unemployment, sickness, disability, widowhood, old age or other lack of livelihood in circumstances beyond his control.

(2) Motherhood and childhood are entitled to special care and assistance. All children, whether born in or out of wedlock, shall enjoy the same social protection.

UNITED NATIONS DEPARTMENT OF PUBLIC INFORMATION/WIKIPEDIA.ORG

DENSITY FACT:
Experts predict that by 2030, 47 percent of people will be living in areas of high water stress.

Tractor spraying pesticides on soybean crop. DUSAN KOSTIC/DREAMSTIME.COM

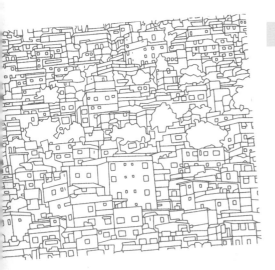

RUNNING DRY

Overpopulation has other consequences. The Colorado and Rio Grande Rivers in the United States, the Yellow River in China and the Indus and Ganges Rivers in South Asia no longer reach the sea. So much of their water is being used for *irrigation*, *urban development* and *hydroelectric energy*, there is none left to flow back into the ocean.

We are also losing our farmland: scientists say we have lost a third of our *arable* land (land suitable for growing crops) in the past forty years. It's not just that people are building on land that could be used for farming. It's also that farmlands are being used so intensely their soil is losing its nutrients. Farmers are forced to use more and more artificial fertilizers and pesticides, causing the soil to degrade until it can no longer grow plants. Degraded soils are more vulnerable to erosion, and topsoil often ends up in rivers, causing water pollution.

Loss of clean water and lack of access to food are issues that people around the world are already struggling with. Today nearly one billion people don't have access to clean drinking water, and countries in South Asia, the Near East and North Africa have no more land left to cultivate.

THAT'S NOT FAIR

People don't suffer equally from these problems. All around the world, poor people suffer from the environmental and social problems caused by overpopulation more than their richer neighbors do. As cities become more crowded, poor people are forced to live in *slums* and in overcrowded housing that is often built on areas where rich people don't want to live, like the sides of mountains or in swamps. The result is that poor people are more likely to be affected by floods and erosion.

When my family and I were in El Salvador in 2001 there was a huge earthquake, and a whole neighborhood of poor

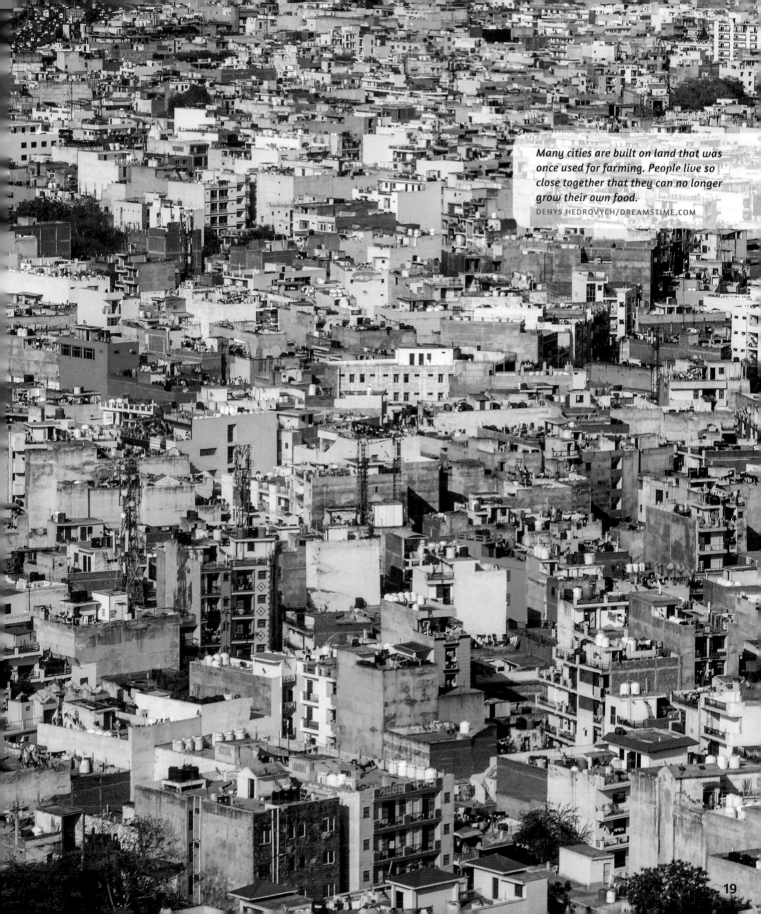

Many cities are built on land that was once used for farming. People live so close together that they can no longer grow their own food.
DENYS HEDROVYCH/DREAMSTIME.COM

Dumping garbage is harmful to people and animals as well as to the environment.
MUAN SIMTE/DREAMSTIME.COM

DENSITY FACT: The United Nations says that since 1990 there have been at least 18 conflicts in which the use (or abuse) of natural resources was an issue.

Shortages of food force people in Venezuela to line up for their rations.
PICCAYA/DREAMSTIME.COM

families' houses was washed off a hillside into the mud below. Many people lost their lives. In 2010 almost one fifth of the country of Pakistan was flooded. The floods were caused by heavy rainfall but were made worse by the massive amount of deforestation in the area on which people's houses were built. Over 1,500 people lost their lives.

KEEP YOUR HANDS OFF!

Today many countries face growing shortages of resources such as water, arable land, forests and fisheries. Overuse of natural resources combined with *environmental degradation*, population growth and climate change pose threats to *human security*. When different groups of people want access to and control over the same resource, conflict can arise, especially when the competing groups already don't get along. If one group of people has traditionally used a field to grow food and then another, more powerful group comes along and says it needs the field for an airport, you can see how the first group might be upset. These kinds of disagreements often lead to conflict. In recent years the people of Sudan, Afghanistan, Sierra Leone, Haiti and many other places have suffered through conflicts fueled partly by scarcity of resources.

GAME ON

Poor people suffer most when conflicts arise, especially if the conflict leads to war. War increases the cost of food and restricts access to water, health care and education. War also disrupts work, so people can't afford to pay their rent. People who were not poor before war started often become poor because they lose their jobs.

Numerous people choose or are forced to leave conflict areas so that they and their families can be safe. Most *refugees* and *immigrants* move to cities, where they can find housing, schools for their kids and medical care. They often settle near people from their country of origin. In some places, such as France and Italy, this influx of new people has put pressure on the existing resources, and there has been a lot of conflict between the people already living in the country and the people arriving. People fleeing such places as Syria, Jordan and Iraq may face racism and hatred from people in the country they have fled to.

In 2018 the Trump administration in the United States ordered a crackdown on immigrants and refugees trying to cross the border between Mexico and the US. Adults crossing the border without papers were charged as criminals and held for questioning. More than 2,000 children were separated from their parents and sent to foster homes and detention centers without knowing when or even if they would see their parents again. The United Nations and several foreign governments called for this practice to end. On June 26, 2018, a federal court judge ordered that the government stop separating families at the border, but several months later over 500 immigrant children had yet to be reunited with their parents.

What's the Difference?

People leave their homes for different reasons. Those who are forced to leave their country to escape war, persecution or a natural disaster are refugees. People who move from place to place in search of seasonal work, like harvesting crops, are known as migrants. People who voluntarily leave their homes and move to another country, often to improve their standard of living, are called emigrants when they leave their home country and immigrants when they arrive in a new country.

Shared Lives

Recently I joined a refugee support group to bring a family to Canada from Uganda. Our role is to raise money to help them settle in Victoria when they get here. We will not only look for a place for them to live, but also help them settle into the community. We will work with them to find schools, figure out where to buy food, show them where the nicest parks are and answer any questions we can. We have learned that the whole family likes to ride bikes, so right now we are holding writing workshops to raise money to buy bikes for them. I hope we get the sizes right!

Biking is a great way to get to know a new city. KARI JONES

Playing soccer together helps these refugee kids in New Zealand feel at home. TIM DOBSON

Fortunately, it is not always this way. People are often happy to provide a new home for those less fortunate than themselves. An organization in Auckland, New Zealand, called Refugees as Survivors New Zealand (RASNZ) decided that one way to help refugees feel at home was to play soccer with them. Soccer is played in many countries, so lots of refugees coming to New Zealand are as crazy about the game as New Zealanders are. The "All Refs" soccer teams for girls and boys help refugees feel like they are part of their new city. Plus, everyone gets to play soccer!

In my own city of Victoria, British Columbia, many refugees from Syria, Uganda and other countries have been welcomed into our schools, workplaces and communities.

In some places, like this refugee camp in Greece, families live in tents while they are waiting for permanent refugee status. DINOSMICHAIL/ISTOCK.COM

A BETTER LIFE

When my father was five years old he emigrated from India to England, and in 1955, when he was fifteen, he came to Canada with his family. He was lucky because he already spoke English, and his family had relatives in Ontario to help them settle in. But not everyone is that lucky. Nearly 1 in 100 people in the world today are refugees. There are currently over 65 million people worldwide being forced to leave their homes to escape overcrowding, disease, famine, flooding, lack of clean water, war and other consequences of overpopulation.

Though life is hard for refugees, many also see a bright future, like these girls who are working hard to keep up with their studies while in a refugee camp in Greece.
FILIPPO GRANDI/SHUTTERSTOCK.COM

'WARRIOR UP'

These problems don't happen only in other countries. When settlers followed the explorers to the Americas from Europe in the 1500s and 1600s, they encountered people already living on these lands. Instead of recognizing that these lands were already home to whole nations, the *colonizers* attacked the Indigenous people and forced them off their ancestral lands. As a result, the surviving Indigenous people had to live in areas set aside for them called *reserves* in Canada and *reservations* in the United States. Indigenous children were taken from their families and sent to *residential schools or Indian day schools,* where they were forced to abandon their traditions, language and culture. When these kids finished school and went back to their homes and communities, they often had trouble fitting in. As a result, their own children suffered; the legacy of residential schools has affected many generations of Indigenous families.

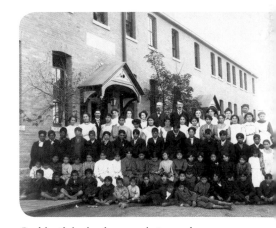

Residential school group photograph, Regina, Saskatchewan, 1908.
LIBRARY AND ARCHIVES CANADA [1] PA-020921/
WIKIPEDIA.ORG

Indigenous people across Canada and the United States still suffer from the effects of colonization. Many Indigenous people live in poverty, which means they don't have adequate housing, access to education, employment or even clean water. Think about how many times a day you turn on the tap and pour

DENSITY FACT: The United Nations estimates that there are 2.1 billion people in the world today who lack access to clean drinking water.

Autumn Peltier has demanded that the leaders of our country ensure all communities have safe drinking water.
LINDA ROY

yourself a drink. People living on some of Canada's reserves can't do that. They have to boil water before they can drink it.

Indigenous people are demanding change. On March 22, 2018, thirteen-year-old Autumn Peltier, an Anishinaabe-Kwe from the Wikwemikong Unceded Territory on Manitoulin Island in northern Ontario, stood in front of the United Nations General Assembly and said, "No child should grow up not knowing what clean water is or never knowing what running water is. We all have a right to this water as we need it—not just rich people, all people." Autumn Peltier told the assembly that it's time to "warrior up" and put an end to this injustice.

LIBRARIES TO THE RESCUE

Helping people overcome poverty is one of the best ways to ensure equality for all. People with education have access to better jobs, which means they have higher incomes and can choose where they live. People who are educated are less likely to suffer the long-term consequences of conflict. They also usually have access to clean water, affordable food and adequate housing.

Educating people starts with teaching them to read, and teaching people to read starts with having libraries full of books and librarians to help. So really, librarians and teachers are superheroes. They are helping to change the world.

In South Africa school libraries are helping to change the lives of some of the country's youngest citizens. For a long time in South Africa, people were separated under a system called *apartheid.* In this system, if you were a white kid you lived in a nice neighborhood in a city, went to a good school and could go to the doctor when you were sick. If you were a black kid you lived in a separate area called a *township*, where people were very poor and didn't have access to things like education and health care.

The apartheid system ended in 1994, but its legacy remains. Even today there is a big gap between the way people in cities in

South Africa live and the way people in the townships live. In the city of Memel and the neighboring township of Zamani, people are working hard to change this. Just a few years ago people in the township were still living in shacks with no electricity or running water. Unemployment rates were high, and people had little access to fresh food. Schools were *segregated*, which means that white children and black children went to different schools.

But then some people got together to start an organization called Memel.Global, and because of that project, things have been changing. Memel.Global started libraries in the area's schools. Kids who have access to books have brighter futures, and now there are over 5,000 books in the school library. Memel. Global also works with families, especially grandmothers, to create kitchen gardens so that everyone has fresh, healthy food to eat. Reading and good food. What could be better?

These kids now have access to whole worlds through the books in their library.
MARLEY HAUSER

Shared Lives

When I was a kid my family lived in Ghana for a few years. Often there was no running water, and people had to line up at the city pumps with buckets and pails. Once, when I was in line with a friend, we saw a woman arrive with three pails, each the size of a water cooler. She filled all three buckets and lined them up on the ground. Then she adjusted her headscarf, raised one bucket onto her head and, without spilling any water, bent over and picked up the other two buckets, one in each hand, and walked away.

Balancing something heavy on your head is much harder than I thought it would be.
MICHAEL PARDY

CHAPTER THREE

Whose World Is This?

NO VACANCY

People aren't the only ones suffering the effects of human overpopulation. With almost eight billion people alive today, finding space to live is tricky whether you're human or not. Around the world, people traditionally lived near rivers or coastlines. Over time people built cities in valleys, on the sides of mountains, in grasslands or forests and even at the edges of deserts. Places that people once avoided, such as the sides of volcanoes (like Auckland, New Zealand, and Mexico City) or the middle of swamps (Chicago and New Orleans), have long since been built over.

Unfortunately, over the past few centuries humans have taken up so much land that other species now struggle to find anywhere suitable to live. Some species that used to run wild across vast lands now have so little area to live in that it's hard for them to feed themselves. A recent study of fifty-seven different species, from field mice to elephants, found that

Wild young camel walking alone in the city of Sharm El Sheikh, Egypt.
PRESSFOTO/DREAMSTIME.COM

animals are much less likely to roam in areas that have been altered by humans. This impacts their ability to find food, water and shelter, which in turn affects their ability to stay alive. Loss of habitat is one of the biggest causes of animal extinction.

In 1980, when I was twelve years old, I went on safari in Kenya with my family. In Amboseli National Park we encountered a herd of over 200 elephants roaming across the land in search of water. In the years since then, there has been so much human activity in elephant habitats that only a fraction of the herd we saw is now left. There were 10 million elephants in 1900, 1.2 million in 1980 and less than half a million in 2018. There are still many stresses on elephant populations, but fortunately there are organizations working hard to bring back these populations, and some herds are growing in number again.

In South America forests are cut down to create grazing lands for cattle. Experts say that we are losing about 80,000 acres of tropical rainforest *a day*, along with 135 plant, animal and insect species.

Farmers in Brazil and around the world have cut down forests to create grazing lands for cattle. This has displaced countless numbers of species. FRONTPAGE/SHUTTERSTOCK.COM

Elephants from the Pinnawala Elephant Orphanage in Sri Lanka walk through the streets of the city every day. Baby elephants cannot survive on their own in the wild if their mothers are injured or killed. CARSTEN BRANDT/ISTOCK.COM

Human activity affects animals even in places where there aren't a lot of people, like the Arctic. Polar bear populations have dropped alarmingly in the last few decades because global climate change is melting the ice they live on.

Wetlands are some of the most productive ecosystems in the world, and there are so many of them that if they were all put together they would take up more space than the entire United States. But they are also vulnerable to human activity, and they are being drained and built over.

All this human activity has had a huge impact on the nonhuman species of the world. The World Wildlife Fund reports that animals are going extinct at a rate 100 to 1,000 times higher than is natural. It has concluded that the populations of fish, birds, mammals, amphibians and reptiles declined by 58 percent between 1970 and 2012. This means that if there were a thousand animals of a particular species in 1970, there are only 420 of them now.

A polar bear managed to get on one of the last ice floes floating in the Arctic Ocean.
RITESH CHAUDHARY/SHUTTERSTOCK.COM

MOVE OVER

There is so much human activity in the world today that other species are struggling to stay alive. In chapter 1 you read about the domestication of animals and how that was beneficial for both humans and other species. But over time we humans have forgotten that we are also members of the animal kingdom. We act as if it doesn't matter what happens to other animals or to the world itself. We act as if the world is ours to do what we want with. If we want to pave a wetland, we do. If we want to cut down a forest, we do. We have forgotten that when you share the world with other living beings, you need to take care of them and make sure their needs are met.

Thank goodness there are many people who know that the world is ours to share, not ours to destroy.

Understanding our place in the world starts with knowing about the species that live around us.
BRUCE KIRKBY

CAMPING WITH SEA WOLVES

Sometimes sharing with nonhuman animals is about setting boundaries. For three months each summer Morgan Pinel and his parents run a kayaking camp on Spring Island, off the west coast of Vancouver Island. But the people are not the island's only inhabitants. For the past several years it has also been home to a family of wolves. When Morgan and his family first discovered there were wolves living on the island, they had to think about how to share the land with them. Morgan's family realized that wolves and people need different things from the land, so they could probably live on the same island peacefully.

Whenever a wolf wanders into camp, Morgan and others in camp shout at them and clap loudly. This tells the wolves they are not welcome in the camp itself. But if anyone encounters a wolf patrolling the shoreline for food at dawn or dusk, it's the people's turn to get out of the way.

Sea wolves live along the coast of North America from California to Alaska. They feed on the ocean's bounty and build their dens in the forest.
ROBERT YONE

Who Owns the Land?

Seeing land as something that can be owned and exploited is an idea that early settlers brought with them to North America. Indigenous peoples have a profound spiritual connection to land, water and the creatures that live in the world. Traditional Indigenous cultures are built on keeping the land healthy, not on owning and exploiting it.

When visitors arrive at the camp, Morgan makes sure they understand the rules. He tells people to keep their eyes open, stay away from the wolves and not leave food lying around. He also tells them to tuck away their shoes, because wolf cubs are like puppies: they like chewing on shoes.

So far people and wolves are peacefully coexisting on the island.

A HOWL OF A TIME

It's one thing to share a camp with a family of wolves. It's another to try to farm sheep or cattle in coyote country. For generations farmers and ranchers across North America struggled to keep their animals safe from carnivores, often by shooting the animals they believed were killing their livestock. Consequently, coyote populations decreased so dramatically in some places that the animals became *endangered*.

Shared Lives

One afternoon when I was visiting Spring Island, BC, I stepped out of my tent and saw a wolf standing about three feet away. He looked at me. I looked at him. We were so close I could see the soft, feathery hairs on his belly. We stared at each other for a few seconds. Then I saw the look in his eyes change, as if he had decided I was just a human—nothing to worry about—and he went on his way. It was an amazing experience looking a full-grown wolf in the eye. I felt like somehow we understood each other.

Having a tidy camp is the best way to make sure the wolves stay safe.
KARI JONES

Today coyote populations are increasing again, and many ranchers and farmers are using traditional and innovative ways of sharing the land with them. Coyotes often den in the same place each year, so ranchers can find the den and make sure to keep their livestock away from the area. Some ranchers and farmers keep dogs who patrol the territory, telling the coyotes—who are also canines, after all—to keep out. Farmers used to tie fluttering flags to fences to scare away wolves and coyotes, and this method has been updated and is in use again. Today's flags are attached to electrified fences. Called turbo-fladry, this tool has proved quite effective in keeping livestock safe.

DENSITY FACT:
Scientists and local Indigenous peoples agree that the coastal wolves, known as sea wolves, are the only wolves in North America that have not been forced out of their natural habitat.

FENCES MAKE GOOD NEIGHBORS

Richard Turere's family are Maasai cattle farmers who live near the edge of Nairobi National Park in Kenya. Their challenge was trying to figure out how to share the land with lions. There are no fences surrounding the park, so animals like zebras and wildebeests rove freely across the surrounding lands. That might sound wonderful to us, but to the Maasai people living there it means there are lions around. While lions feed mostly on zebras and other wild animals, they also kill and eat cattle. When lions kill cattle, people kill the lions. In the past twenty years or so, the lion population in Kenya has plummeted from around 15,000 to only 2,000.

One morning when he was thirteen, Richard woke up to find that lions had killed his family's only bull. Losing your bull can be devastating, because it means you have no way of breeding the cattle and keeping the herd growing.

Richard knew he had to do something. In Maasai culture boys take care of their father's cattle, so it was Richard's job to keep them safe. He knew the lion populations were suffering because people and lions were living too close to each other. After a few failures he finally came up with the idea of using

Keeping cattle safe is an important job for many Maasai boys.
ALEKSANDAR TODOROVIC/SHUTTERSTOCK.COM

DENSITY FACT: The citizens of Oslo, Norway, have created a bee highway so that bees can travel safely across the city.

solar panels to power a car battery, which he connected to a switch. That switch turns lights along the cattle pen on and off so that the lions think there is someone walking around in the cattle area. Lions stay away because they have learned to be afraid of humans, who often shoot them. Richard's idea worked so well that other families asked him to install similar setups in their cattle pens, and now this method is being used across Kenya to scare away lions, hyenas, leopards and elephants. This is great news, not only for the cattle farmers, but also for all the wild animals whose lives are being saved by this invention.

HIGHWAYS AND BYWAYS

Because humans have taken over so many places on Earth, many animals have a hard time getting from one place to another. Animals that used to have huge hunting ranges have been pushed into smaller and smaller areas, such as national parks and reserves. But this doesn't always work well for either the humans or the other species. Every year I hear stories on the news about cougars and bears that have wandered into the city in search of food. Almost every time the story ends with the animal being shot. These animals used to have vast forests to forage and hunt in, but my city has grown so much in the past ten years that many of these forests are now gone. Deer have been displaced and have come into the city in large numbers; cougars are simply following their prey.

The city of Oslo is really buzzing with action.
MATTHEW BRYCE/BYBI OSLO

When animals travel from one place to another, maybe to find food or to get away from poachers, they must cross spaces where people live. Cities and agriculture take up so much space that animals have no choice but to creep into backyards and alleyways or, most dangerous of all, to cross highways.

People around the world are trying to solve this problem by creating animal highways so that animals can get where they need to go safely.

DENSITY FACT:
In Moscow about 20 stray dogs have learned how to ride the subway.

The Terai Arc Landscape (TAL), a series of wildlife corridors that connects protected areas from India to Nepal, allows the Bengal tiger, the Asian elephant and the Indian rhino (all three are endangered species) to freely move between the Yamuna River in India and the Bagmati River in Nepal.

On Christmas Island in Australia, residents have built tunnel crossings under their roads, and bridges over them, to allow the famous Christmas Island red crabs to move from the forest to the ocean safely. There are an estimated 50 million red crabs on Christmas Island, and the people who live there do their best to drive slowly and help the crabs along whenever possible.

Overpasses like this allow wildlife to cross highways safely.
PICS-XL/SHUTTERSTOCK.COM

Shared Lives

My mother loves to garden, so when my family moved to Ghana when I was eleven years old, she started digging out a vegetable patch near a tree in our yard. One day a neighbor noticed her digging and ran over to her, yelling and waving. He was trying to warn her that there was a cobra nesting under the tree! My mother sprang back in alarm. She never did build her vegetable bed in that garden, and we kept a sharp eye out for signs of the snake. Even when our friendly neighbor told us it had moved on, we always took a wide path around the tree on our way to the street.

My mother in her gardening clothes.

33

CHAPTER FOUR

Sharing Our Lives

Sharing the world is something we can all take part in. It's not only about changing farming practices or protecting arable land. It's also about how we pay attention to the land we live on and the people and animals around us. As the world's population grows, we need to ask ourselves, What is my fair share, and how can I help others get their fair share? We need to think about how we can change our own attitudes and lifestyles to make the world a better place for other people and other species.

SHARING AT HOME

What does sharing mean for us in our own homes?

Is there a way you can eat food that has a smaller impact on the environment? Eating a low-impact diet means eating food that is grown locally and eating less meat (or none at all). The farther food travels, the greater its environmental impact. The more meat we eat, the more land has to be cleared for grazing. (See *Let's Eat!* in this series for more details on food security.)

City planners in Copenhagen designed this park so that everyone, young and old, would be able to use it.
CHARLOTTE AMMUNDSENS PLADS

Helping other species survive in the city can be fun. Get together with friends to make bird feeders out of milk and juice bottles. PAVEL L PHOTO AND VIDEO/ JURATE/SHUTTERSTOCK.COM

Is the tap water in your area safe to drink? Avoiding bottled water keeps a lot of plastic out of the environment. If you don't have tap water you can drink, can you buy water in large containers to cut down on plastic use? (See *Trash Talk* in this series for more about dealing with our garbage.)

How do you get around? Do you walk? Take the bus? Bike? These are all forms of transport that have a low impact on the environment.

What can your household do to support the other species living in your area? Can you put up a bird feeder or grow some native plants in your yard or in pots? Can you let your grass grow long and stop using pesticides? Can you set up an insect hotel somewhere? (See *Going Wild* in this series for more details on how to support wild creatures in your area.)

Insect hotels help turn our backyards and gardens into vibrant homes for birds, butterflies and other species.
JURATE BUIVIENE/DREAMSTIME.COM

Sharing books with neighbors through Little Libraries is a great way to build community.
LINDA WILLIAMS/DREAMSTIME.COM

Do you know where your clothes come from? Ask your parents to look for fair trade clothing and other goods. (See *A Fair Deal* in this series for more details on fair trade and what it means.)

What happens to your clothing, footwear and sports equipment when you outgrow it? Can you donate it to a local charity? Do you have books you can donate to a local library? Keeping items out of landfills helps to keep the environment healthy, and donating clothing and books in good condition helps others in your community.

SHARING IN THE COMMUNITY

What about sharing outside the home? What can you do to help make your community an easier place for everyone to live in?

Does your community have a food bank, shelter or soup kitchen? Ask your parents if you can volunteer to help feed people less fortunate than you. If that isn't possible, think about how you could raise some money to donate to the food bank.

Are there immigrants or refugees in your community? Most cities have organizations that help newcomers settle into their new homes. Ask your parents to help you find out about local organizations and how to volunteer for them.

Do you live by a river, lake or ocean? Join a beach cleanup. Access to clean drinking water starts with taking care of our beaches and shorelines.

Are there parks nearby? Many parks have volunteers who help keep the trails safe and clean.

SHARING AT SCHOOL

Schools are an important part of the sharing equation.

Does your school have a social justice club? If not, start one! School clubs can raise awareness through field trips, posters, display tables, bake sales, film nights and other activities.

Beach cleanups help keep both the oceans and our beaches free of plastic and other garbage.
YACOBCHUK/ISTOCK.COM

Building community starts at school. Make friends and take action. SHUTTERSTOCK.COM

Shared Lives

Recently my son decided to become a vegan (a person who does not eat or use animal products). Initially I found it hard to cook for him because I'm not used to cooking that way. The first time I made him a meal, I messed up and used milk. Then my son showed me a few recipes he has used, and now I've got the hang of it. My favorite vegan dish is guacamole with cucumbers and fresh tomatoes. Now that I'm making vegan meals for my son, I'm also eating less meat and other animal products. I'm proud of him for making this choice and learning how to eat a healthy, vegan diet and for helping me to start eating that way too.

Rowan loves to cook vegan food
KARI JONES

Present what you learn about the issues in your area to the rest of the school and to your city council.

Does your school have a garden? Volunteer to help dig in the dirt. Use the garden to grow food for you and your classmates. Any extra fresh produce can be donated to the local soup kitchen or shelter. If your school has a kitchen, ask about making it a fair trade kitchen.

Remember how important education is to helping people overcome poverty. Can you help younger kids learn how to read, either at your own school or in a refugee and immigrant center in your area?

SHARING WITH FRIENDS AND THE WORLD

Share with the world! There are so many ways to make change. Here are a few suggestions.

Get artsy. Music, painting, writing, sculpture, dance and videos can all be used to create awareness of important issues. In 2017 school kids from the Blueberry River First Nations in northeastern British Columbia worked with an organization called N'we Jinan to make a music video called "Where Happiness Dwells." The lyrics speak about how their community struggles with violence and teen suicide and how the kids have hope that they can overcome these problems. They posted their video to YouTube, and now people everywhere can hear their voices.

Do some research. Learning about the place where you live is an important step in sharing the world well. Do a Google search, and ask your parents, grandparents, teachers and librarians what they know about the history of your area. Whose traditional lands do you live on? What language do the Indigenous people in your region speak? What do their traditional houses look like? Do they hunt, fish or farm? What is their relationship with the animals in their territory? Where are the Indigenous people from your area living now? Many Indigenous peoples of North America

School kids learn how to grow healthy food through their school gardening program.
KRYZHOV/SHUTTERSTOCK.COM

are no longer living in their traditional territories, but have been relocated to reserves. Knowing something about the people whose land we live on is part of restoring justice and sharing the world more equally.

Learn from your elders. Communities in the Great Bear Rainforest on the coast of British Columbia benefit from a program called SEAS—Supporting Emerging Aboriginal Stewards. SEAS works with Indigenous students to help them learn about the lands and waters of their traditional territories. Elders from each community spend time with students and teach them traditional ways of being. One of the goals of the program is to help kids see that they are part of their environment, so they will be inspired to take care of it just the way their ancestors did over many centuries. Last summer a group of elders and students took a trip along the coast to learn about gathering mtm (sea urchins). They learned how to identify them, dive for them and cook them. They also learned that it is important to leave some behind, because mtm are part of the ecosystem, which is only healthy when all its parts are in balance. By learning these things, the students are studying the traditions of their people. For them, as for many people, understanding and honoring their traditional ways means understanding that the world around them is part of who they are. With this understanding also comes knowledge of how to share the world around them with the animals and ecosystems they live among.

Join activist Autumn Peltier in her fight to bring clean drinking water to all of our communities. You don't have to be famous, and you don't have to speak in front of the United Nations to be heard. Talk to your classmates and others in your community. If you are part of a faith-based organization such as a church, temple, mosque or synagogue, share your knowledge there. To learn more about water issues, join Wavemakers, a project of the Centre for Affordable Water and Sanitation Technology in Canada, or The Water Project in the United States.

N'we Jinan Artists wrote their song "Where Happiness Dwells" to help raise awareness of community issues. ANDREI SAVU

Learning from elders makes a community strong. PHIL CHARLES/SEAS.ORG

Malala has inspired youth around the world to take action by speaking out on issues important to them.
SOUTHBANK CENTRE/WIKIPEDIA.ORG

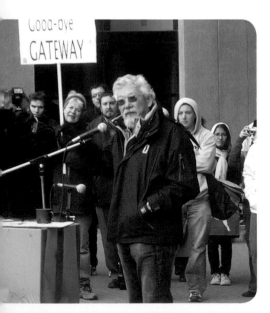

At the Day of Global Action in Vancouver in 2007, David Suzuki spoke to the audience about the importance of taking action on the environment. WIKIPEDIA COMMONS

BE INSPIRED!

Doing research for this book made me realize how many kids out there are making a difference in the world. Here are just a few.

Malala Yousafzai has changed the world. She has brought awareness of the importance of education for girls to all of our homes. My friend Mira, who is fourteen, was inspired by Malala and has started raising awareness of the importance of education. She makes bookmarks with sayings about education on them and sells them at a table on her street. She donates the money she raises to an agency that sends girls to school. She also talks to kids at her school about fair trade, and she's part of a leadership club. These things are all about making sure we share the world more fairly.

In my city some of our most active citizens are kids. Franny and her brother Rupert were only six and ten when they first became activists. It started when Rupert went to hear David Suzuki talk about his Blue Dot initiative, which states that our right to breathe clean air, drink clean water and eat safe food should be legally recognized at all levels of government. At the end of the talk David Suzuki called on everyone in the audience to ask their governments to help. Rupert decided that when David Suzuki said *everyone,* he meant Rupert too, even if he wasn't old enough to vote. Rupert and Franny wrote letters to all the government people they could think of. They were invited to city hall to give a presentation to the city councilors, which resulted in the City of Victoria getting on board. Since then Rupert and Franny have worked hard to build the city they want to live in. For Franny, that means having more public art and gardens. For Rupert, it means helping everyone value the environment. Franny says, "You thrive more with community," and Rupert says, "The more people who get on board, the more change we can make."

Twins Jake and Max Klein spent a lot of time looking for ways to volunteer but kept being turned down because they were too young. They didn't give up: when they were thirteen they started an online database called Kids That Do Good, which links kids with volunteer opportunities like helping the homeless, serving Thanksgiving dinner at seniors homes or working with injured animals. Jake and Max search for organizations that welcome kid volunteers. Kids can search the site for opportunities all across the United States.

The Klein twins aren't the only kids to start their own organization. Abbie and Riley Weeks, both students at Cherry Creek High School in Greenwood Village, Colorado, created a nonprofit organization called Ecological Action, which is dedicated to encouraging sustainable practices. In 2016 they installed panels to provide solar energy to a school in Uganda. In 2017 they partnered with another nonprofit called GRID Alternatives to install solar panels on a resident's house on the Pine Ridge Reservation in South Dakota. Their teacher calls these kids solar warriors.

Rupert and Franny are leaders in their community, acting for the environment and their city. SKYE LADELL

Boyan Slat's nonprofit organization Ocean Cleanup hopes to get rid of 50 percent of the Great Pacific Garbage Patch in just five years.
THE OCEAN CLEANUP

In 2011, when he was sixteen, Boyan Slat was diving in Greece when he realized there was more plastic in the sea than fish. He decided to dedicate his time to cleaning up the ocean. In 2013 he founded The Ocean Cleanup, with the goal of clearing the ocean of plastics. His system harnesses ocean currents to concentrate plastic in one place where it can be gathered and removed from the water. The first prototype was deployed in 2016, and in September 2018 he launched a full-scale operation. Boyan Slat was the youngest ever recipient of the United Nations Environment Programme's Champions of the Earth award in 2014.

These kids were all ordinary people living ordinary lives until they decided to be part of creating change. Making the world a great place to live for all of us is about remembering we are part of a huge web of life that works best when all its parts are taken care of. We all have a role to play, whether we are young or old, rich or poor. If we live our lives with compassion for those around us and remember that all it takes to make a difference is to act, surely we can change the world!

In the township of Memel, South Africa, kids play sports at school. MARLEY HAUSER

Acknowledgments

Some books are easy and quick to write, and others take a lot of time and thought. This one took me a long time and required a lot of help. Thank you especially to Michael Pardy for listening to me talk about this book in its many forms and for helping me sort out my ideas. Thank you also to Robin Stevenson, who sat across the table from me and kept me going over the many hours we spent writing together. Of course, I also want to thank the Wildwood Writers: Laurie Elmquist, Julie Paul and Alisa Gordaneer. Where would I be without you all?

Many people around the world gave me their time and lots of information. Thank you to Dave, Caroline and Morgan Pinel, Richard Turere, Mike Reid, Skye, Franny and Rupert, Mira, Autumn Peltier and all the others who let me write about them and use their photos.

This book was just words on a page until Sarah Harvey helped me fine-tune it and Jenn Playford added all the wonderful photos and design. Thank you to both of you and to all the other members of the team at Orca Book Publishers.

Finally, thank you to my family for all your love and support. I am what I am because of you.

Resources

Print

Jones, Kari. *A Fair Deal: Shopping for Social Justice.* Victoria, BC: Orca Book Publishers, 2017.

McLaughlin, Danielle. *That's Not Fair!: Getting to Know Your Rights and Freedoms.* Toronto, ON: Kids Can Press, 2016.

Mulder, Michelle. *Going Wild: Helping Nature Thrive in Cities.* Victoria, BC: Orca Book Publishers, 2018.

Mulder, Michelle. *Trash Talk: Moving Toward a Zero-Waste World.* Victoria, BC: Orca Book Publishers, 2015.

Smith, David. *If the World Were a Village.* Toronto, ON: Kids Can Press, 2011.

Spilsbury, Louise. *Poverty and Hunger.* Hauppauge, NY: Barron's Educational Series, 2017.

Strauss, Rochelle. *One Well: The Story of Water on Earth.* Toronto, ON: Kids Can Press, 2007.

Suzuki, David, and Kathy Vanderlinden. *You Are the Earth: Know Your World So You Can Help Make It Better.* Vancouver, BC: Greystone Books/David Suzuki Foundation, 2010.

Tate, Nikki. *Better Together: Creating Community in an Uncertain World.* Victoria, BC: Orca Book Publishers, 2018.

Veness, Kimberly. *Let's Eat!: Sustainable Food for a Hungry Planet.* Victoria, BC: Orca Book Publishers, 2017.

Online

Children's International Summer Villages: cisv.org

Ecological Action: ecologicalaction.org

Kids That Do Good: kidsthatdogood.com

Me to We: we.org

OXFAM: oxfam.org/en/countries/volunteer-us

Scouts International: scout.org.

Wavemakers (Centre for Affordable Water and Sanitation Technology): cawst.org/wavemakers

The Water Project: thewaterproject.org

Links to external resources are for personal and/or educational use only and are provided in good faith without any express or implied warranty. There is no guarantee given as to the accuracy or currency of any individual item. Orca Book Publishers provides links as a service to readers. This does not imply any endorsement by Orca Book Publishers of any of the content accessed through these links.

Glossary

apartheid—a policy that separated and discriminated against nonwhite groups in the Republic of South Africa

arable—fit for growing crops

biodiversity—the variety of plant and animal life in the world or in a particular ecosystem

colonizer—someone who establishes a colony or settles in a new place

conservationist—someone who advocates for the protection and preservation of the environment and wildlife

domesticated—having adapted over time from being wild to living in close association with humans

endangered (species)—at risk of becoming extinct

environmental degradation—a process through which an environment is damaged

human security—freedom from such threats as poverty, disease and violence and having access to such things as food and clean drinking water

hydroelectric energy—electricity produced by the movement of water

immigrant—a person who comes to a country to take up permanent residence

Indigenous peoples—the original inhabitants of a region or country

Industrial Revolution—the shift to new manufacturing processes whereby machines made products that people had always made by hand; it took place from 1760 to sometime between 1820 and 1840

irrigation—supplying water to crops or land, usually by diverting water from a river

refugee—a person who has been forced to leave their country in order to escape war, persecution or a natural disaster

reservations (US)/**reserves** (Canada)—land put aside by federal governments for Indigenous peoples to live on, often far from those peoples' traditional territories

residential schools or Indian day schools—government-sponsored schools (run by the federal government in conjunction with religious organizations) that were meant to assimilate Indigenous children into the settler population

segregated—separated or set apart from others on the basis of race

slums—densely populated urban areas in which housing is inadequate and people often don't have access to clean water, proper sanitation and other services

township—in South Africa, a suburb or city of predominantly black occupation

urban development—developing or improving an area by building on it

Index

Page numbers in **bold** indicate an image caption.

Index (continued)

Jefferson Madison Regional Library
201 E Market Street
Charlottesville, VA 22902